Dr Jekyll and Mr Hyde

by Robert Louis Stevenson

retold by Jenny Alexander

Robert Louis Stevenson (1850–94) grew up in Edinburgh. He studied law at university, but then decided to be a writer.

In his early twenties, he developed a weak chest. He went to live in Samoa, to get away from the cold Scottish climate. His first book was <u>Treasure Island</u> (1883). The idea for <u>Dr Jekyll and Mr Hyde</u> came to him in a dream.

~1~
The Door

Mr Utterson the lawyer was a tall, thin man, who hardly ever smiled. He had few friends except his family and people he had known since his school days.

Every Sunday, he and his cousin, Mr Richard Enfield, went for a walk together. One day, they passed a sinister-looking building. It was two storeys high, with no windows and only a small door. The door had no bell or knocker, and the paint was stained and peeling.

"That door," said Mr Enfield, "reminds me of a very strange story. It happened like this.

Dr Jekyll & Mr Hyde

"I was walking home late one night, when a girl of about eight or nine came running out of a side street and crashed into a man who was walking past the corner. To my surprise, the man turned and stamped on her as she lay on the ground. I shouted at him and he ran away.

"I went after him and brought him back. Several people had gathered around the girl, who was still lying on the ground.

4

Dr Jekyll & Mr Hyde

"They wanted to give the man a beating, but I said it would be better to make him pay the girl some money. He agreed to pay £100, and brought us here to this door. He went inside, and came back with £10 in cash and a cheque for the other £90. The cheque was not signed by himself, but by a gentleman we both know. I asked myself, 'Why should a respectable man want to pay the debts of a villain?' The only thing I could think of was that the wretch had some kind of hold over him."

Mr Utterson wanted to know who had written the cheque, but Enfield would not tell him. He would only say that the villain's name was Mr Edward Hyde.

~2~
The Search for Mr Hyde

Mr Utterson had heard the name Edward Hyde before, and he thought he could guess who had written the cheque for him. He had drawn up a will for his old friend, Dr Henry Jekyll, which said, "If I should die or disappear, I leave everything to Mr Edward Hyde." Mr Utterson felt worried at the time because he didn't know anything about Mr Hyde. Now he felt even worse.

He decided to make Mr Hyde tell him what was going on. "If he be Mr Hyde," he said to himself, "I shall be Mr Seek."

Dr Jekyll & Mr Hyde

Mr Utterson hung around outside Hyde's house. At last, he saw a small man go up to the door and take a key out of his pocket. Mr Utterson went up to him and touched the man's arm.

The man pulled his arm away. He was very short, and his clothes were too big for him. "Mr Hyde?" said Utterson. "That is my name," the man said, in a sneering way. "What do you want?"

Mr Utterson had to make an effort to be polite. "I am a friend of Dr Jekyll," he said. "Would you like to ask me in?" Mr Hyde laughed in his face. He went inside and shut the door without another word.

As Mr Hyde would not speak to him, Utterson decided he would have to make Dr Jekyll tell him what was going on. He went to Jekyll's house. The door was opened by his Jekyll's butler, Poole. Dr Jekyll was not at home, so Utterson asked Poole whether he knew Mr Hyde. The butler told him Mr Hyde was often at the house; he had his own key, and the servants had orders to obey him.

"But I have never met him here," said Utterson.

"That is because he comes and goes through the laboratory," said Poole.

Utterson didn't like the idea of that evil little rat of a man coming and going secretly around the back of the doctor's house.

~3~
The Carew Murder

Dr Jekyll refused to talk about Mr Hyde, and Mr Utterson had to let the matter drop. But then something terrible happened. One of Mr Utterson's clients, Sir Danvers Carew, was beaten to death in the street by a man with a heavy walking stick. A witness recognised the murderer as Mr Hyde.

Dr Jekyll & Mr Hyde

Mr Utterson went to the police and offered to show them where Mr Hyde lived. He took them to Mr Hyde's house, and knocked on the door.

Mr Hyde was not at home. He seemed to have left in a hurry. His rooms were very untidy. There were ashes in the grate, with scraps of paper and part of a green cheque book among them.

Behind the door, Utterson found a bloodstained walking stick. It was one he had given to Dr Jekyll some years before.

~4~
The Letter

Dr Jekyll & Mr Hyde

Mr Utterson went to see Dr Jekyll. Poole took him through the back garden to the laboratory, where the doctor had his study. It was a small room with three windows that looked out onto a courtyard. Dr Jekyll was sitting by the fire. He looked sick.

"Have you heard the news?" said Utterson. "Your friend killed Carew. Tell me you are not stupid enough to be hiding him."

Dr Jekyll swore he would never see Hyde again. He said he had had a letter from him that very morning. He showed it to Utterson.

> My dear Jekyll,
> I am sorry I have behaved so badly in spite of everything you have done for me. I am going away, and shall never ask for your help again.
> Your friend,
> Edward Hyde

Mr Utterson was glad. However, on his way out, he asked Poole about the messenger who had brought the letter. Poole said there had not been any messengers to the house that day.

Dr Jekyll
& Mr Hyde

Mr Utterson wondered why Dr Jekyll had lied to him. As soon as he got home, he read the letter again. The handwriting looked familiar. Mr Utterson got Dr Jekyll's latest dinner invitation and laid it on the desk next to Hyde's letter. The handwriting was almost exactly the same, except that it was slanted differently.

Mr Utterson groaned. Why would his dear friend Dr Jekyll want to forge a letter for a murderer?

*My dear Jekyll,
I am sorry I have behaved so badly in spite of everything you have done for me. I am going away and shall never ask for your help again.
Your friend,
Edward Hyde*

*Dear Utterson,
I cordially invite you to a dinner party on Friday at 7.30pm
Your friend,
Jekyll*

~5~
The Window

The police searched for Mr Hyde, but he had gone. For a while, Dr Jekyll became more like his old self. He was more friendly and less secretive. Utterson hoped they could put the past behind them. But then Jekyll started refusing to see anyone. He said he needed to be on his own.

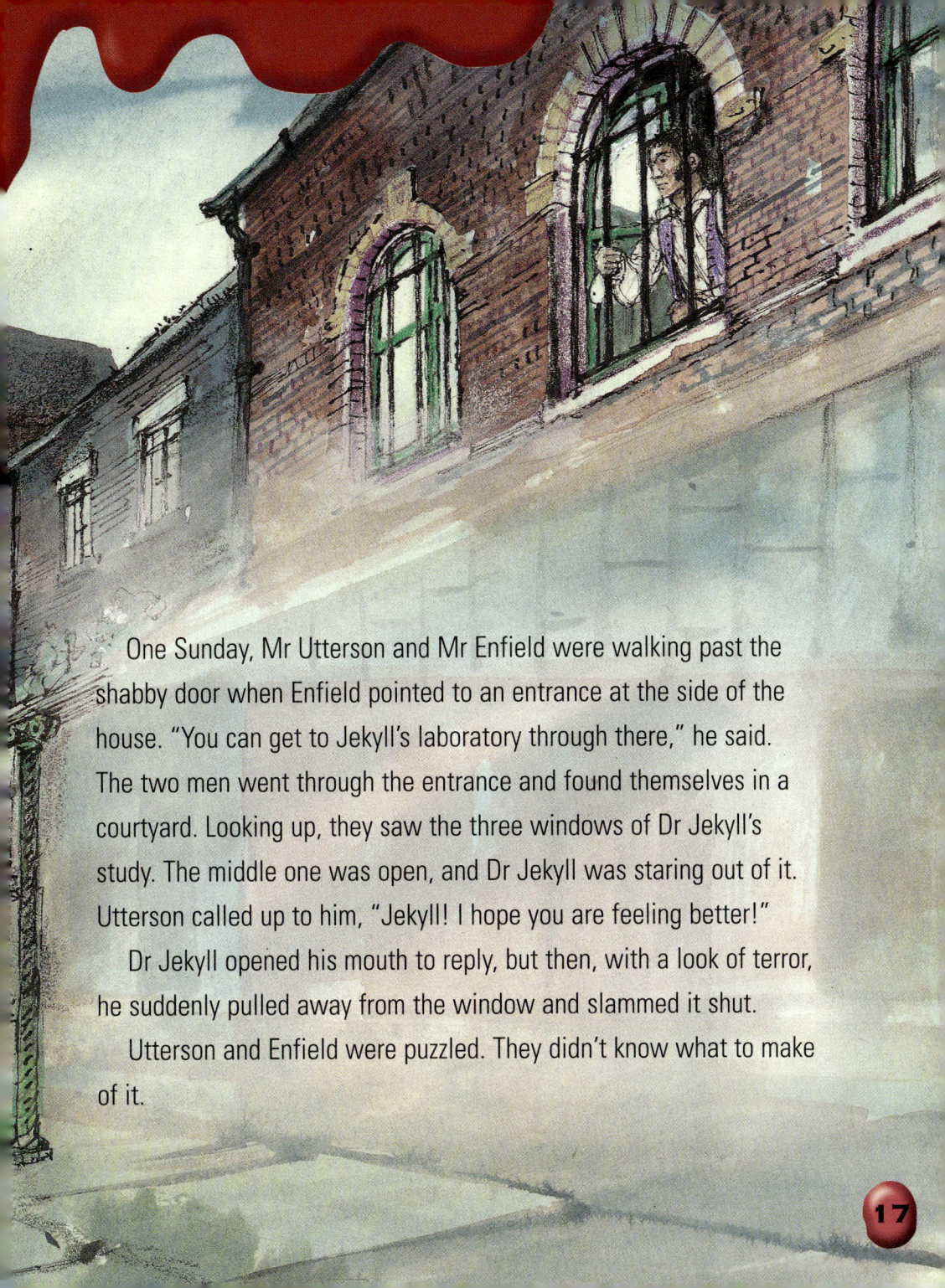

One Sunday, Mr Utterson and Mr Enfield were walking past the shabby door when Enfield pointed to an entrance at the side of the house. "You can get to Jekyll's laboratory through there," he said. The two men went through the entrance and found themselves in a courtyard. Looking up, they saw the three windows of Dr Jekyll's study. The middle one was open, and Dr Jekyll was staring out of it. Utterson called up to him, "Jekyll! I hope you are feeling better!"

Dr Jekyll opened his mouth to reply, but then, with a look of terror, he suddenly pulled away from the window and slammed it shut.

Utterson and Enfield were puzzled. They didn't know what to make of it.

~6~
The Last Night

One evening in March, Mr Utterson had a visit from Poole. The butler seemed upset. "Please come with me, sir," he said. "I think there has been foul play." Mr Utterson followed him into the night. He felt full of dread.

When they got to Dr Jekyll's study, Poole knocked on the door. "Mr Utterson is here to see you, sir," he said. They heard a voice from inside say, "Tell him I can't see anyone." Poole led Utterson back down the stairs. "Was that Dr Jekyll's voice?" Utterson demanded. Poole was not sure. "Eight days ago we heard Dr Jekyll scream," Poole said. "No one has seen him since."

Dr Jekyll
& Mr Hyde

19

The servants thought their master had been murdered. But why should the murderer lock himself in the study? And why should he call out for medicine, and leave notes on the stairs for the servants to take to the chemist? Poole had one of the notes in his pocket. He showed it to Utterson.

To Messrs Maw.
The chemicals you keep sending me are not pure enough. I bought the same chemical from you several years ago. Please send me some of the original batch straight away...

Utterson said, "This is Jekyll's handwriting, Poole. What makes you think it isn't the doctor in the study?" Poole answered, "I have seen him. He was in the laboratory. As soon as he saw me, he ran back to the study. If it was my master I saw, why did he have a mask over his face?"

"A mask?" said Utterson. "It's all falling into place! Jekyll has locked himself up in his study because he has developed some embarrassing skin complaint. That's why he keeps sending for medicines. That's why he doesn't want us to see him!"

Poole shook his head. "The man I saw was far too small to be Dr Jekyll... I think it was Mr Hyde."

Utterson got a poker and Poole got an axe. They went to the study. They could hear the sound of footsteps pacing up and down. Utterson knocked on the door, and the pacing stopped.

"Jekyll!" he cried. "Open this door, or we'll break it down."

A voice wailed from inside, "Utterson! Please..."

It wasn't Dr Jekyll's voice. It was Mr Hyde's.

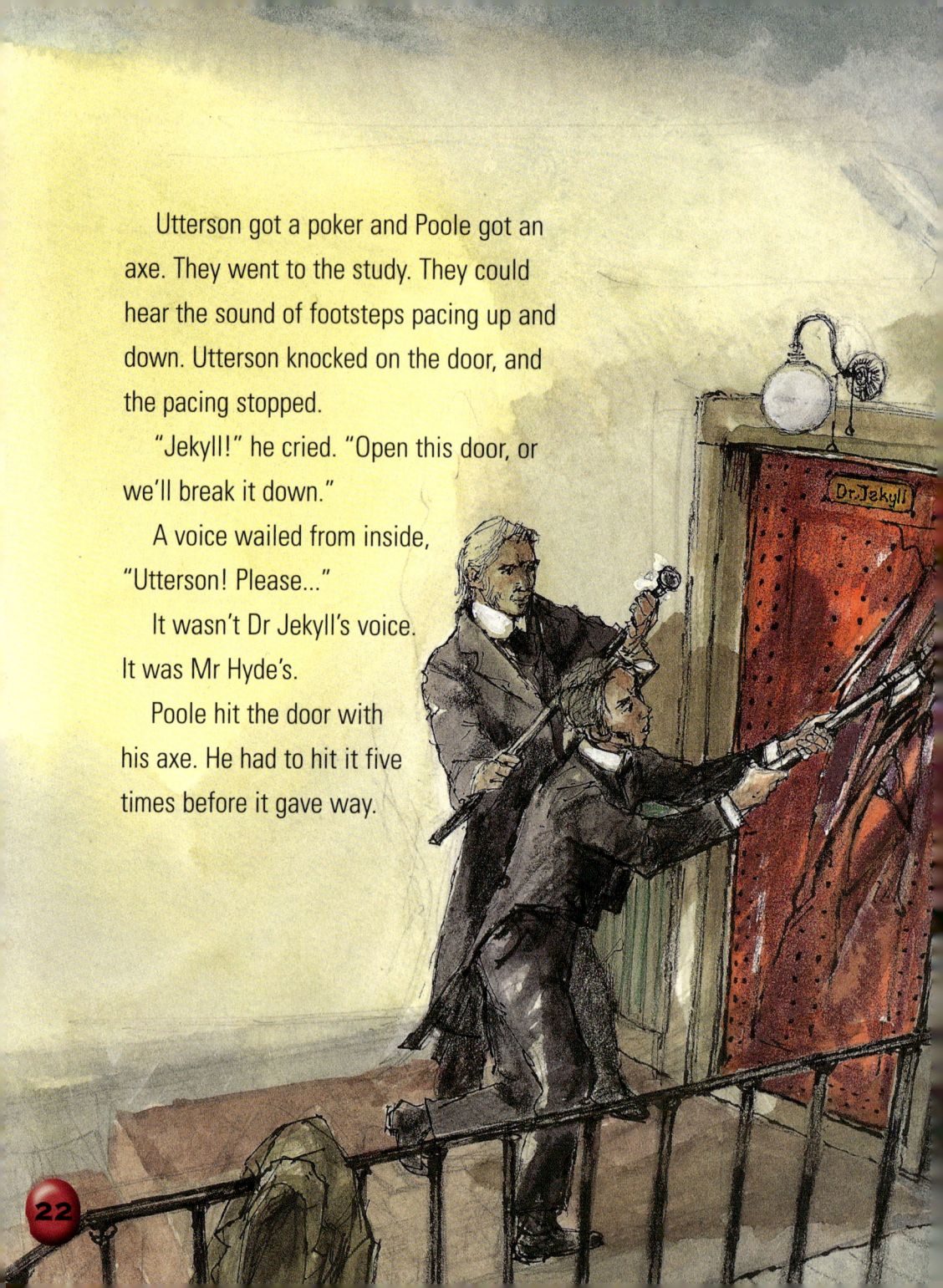

Poole hit the door with his axe. He had to hit it five times before it gave way.

Dr Jekyll & Mr Hyde

The two men found Mr Hyde close to death, with a bottle of poison in his hand. "It is too late for him," said Utterson. "But where is Dr Jekyll?" On the desk there was a large envelope, addressed to Mr Utterson.

There were three things in the envelope. The first was a new will leaving everything to Utterson. The second was a note – "When you read this, I shall have disappeared, although I don't know in what way. If you want to know more, read my confession. From your friend, Henry Jekyll." The third thing was Dr Jekyll's confession.

~7~
Henry Jekyll's Confession

I came from a respectable family, and I wanted to work hard and help other people. But there was always a selfish part of me that only wanted to have fun. Although I tried to resist it, sometimes I couldn't. Then I would go out and get drunk in secret. I started to lead a double life.

I felt like two people sharing one body: a respectable doctor and a drunken reveller. I thought perhaps everybody had a split nature like me – one part that wanted to do good, and the other that wanted to do what it liked. I started to imagine what it would be like if we could actually separate the two.

Dr Jekyll
& Mr Hyde

I already knew from my work that the physical body was not as solid as it seemed. Certain chemicals could cause changes in the flesh and blood, making it tremble like a liquid and dissolve into a mist. I thought it might be possible to dissolve one body and create two, one for the good side of a man's nature and the other for the bad.

Dr Jekyll & Mr Hyde

I knew it would be dangerous to test my theory, but in the end I just had to find out if it would work. So I mixed the chemicals and drank the mixture down.

I felt terrible pains in every part of my body. Waves of sickness and fear went through me. Then suddenly it was over. My body felt younger, lighter and happier. My mind was full of wild ideas, and I wanted to do all kinds of wicked things. But I was smaller than before, probably because I had always shut out the wild side of my nature so much that it was less developed than the good side.

I drank the potion again to see if I could go back to my original form. I felt the same pains and sickness and terror. When it stopped, I was Dr Jekyll again.

I loved the idea of having two separate identities. I called the wild one Mr Hyde, and bought a house for him. I told my servants that a Mr Hyde would be calling from time to time, and they should serve him if I was away. I wrote the will that you objected to so much, in case something went wrong and I couldn't return to the body of Dr Jekyll.

I didn't really want to do anything evil; I just wanted to have some fun. But as soon as I became Mr Hyde, he took over. He liked hurting other people, and his heart was as hard as stone. Sometimes the things he did shocked me, but I told myself it was not me who had done them.

About two months before the murder of Sir Danvers Carew something worrying happened. I went to bed as Dr Jekyll, and woke up as Mr Hyde! How had this come about? What if giving the darker side of my nature a free rein had made it grow too powerful? What if Mr Hyde took over completely? I was frightened. I decided to try to live without Mr Hyde. But after two months, I gave up. I took another dose of the potion.

29

Having been shut out for so long, Mr Hyde was more evil than ever. He killed Sir Danvers Carew, feeling nothing but wicked delight. Then he realised he was in trouble. He had to disappear!

When I was Dr Jekyll again I had to face up to the horror of what I had done. I had created a monster in Mr Hyde. I had done terrible things through him. Now he had gone too far, and I knew I must break free of him forever.

I threw myself into good works, and soon stopped feeling so bad about myself. One day, I even thought, "I am better than other people because I try so hard to do good." At that very moment the pains, the sickness and the terror came. I looked down. My clothes were too big for me. My hands, which are normally large and pale, were small and hairy. They were the hands of Mr Hyde!

After that, every time I fell asleep, I would wake up as Mr Hyde. It happened even if I dozed off for a few seconds. Whenever I changed into Mr Hyde, I needed bigger and bigger doses of the potion to bring me back to Dr Jekyll again.

Then disaster struck! I ran out of the chemical I had used for so long. I sent for more, but I couldn't get the potion to work. Later I found out that the original chemical was impure, and it must have been the impurity that made the potion work.

31

So you see, my days are numbered. I don't know how it will end, but I know that next time I change into Mr Hyde, I will never be able to come back. Perhaps Hyde will die in prison or take his own life. I don't know. In a short time, Dr Jekyll will be no more. As for Mr Hyde, he is a different person.

Here ends the confession and the unhappy life of your poor friend, Henry Jekyll.